GENETIC ENGINEERING

© Aladdin Books Ltd 1991

Designed and produced by
Aladdin Books Ltd
28 Percy Street
London W1P 9FF

First published in 1991
in Great Britain by
Franklin Watts Ltd
96 Leonard Street
London EC2A 4RH

A CIP catalogue record
for this book is
available from the
British Library.

ISBN 0 7496 0411 5

Printed in Belgium

Front cover: A genetic engineer in the laboratory.
Back cover: Computer graphic of the double helix molecule of DNA.

The author, Nigel Hawkes, is science correspondent of *The Times*
newspaper in London.

The consultant, Steve Parker, is a writer and editor in the life sciences,
health and medicine.

Design: Rob Hillier, Andy Wilkinson
Editor: Jen Green
Picture researcher: Emma Krikler
Illustrator: Ron Hayward Associates

Contents

GENETIC ENGINEERING

NIGEL HAWKES

Franklin Watts
London : New York : Toronto : Sydney

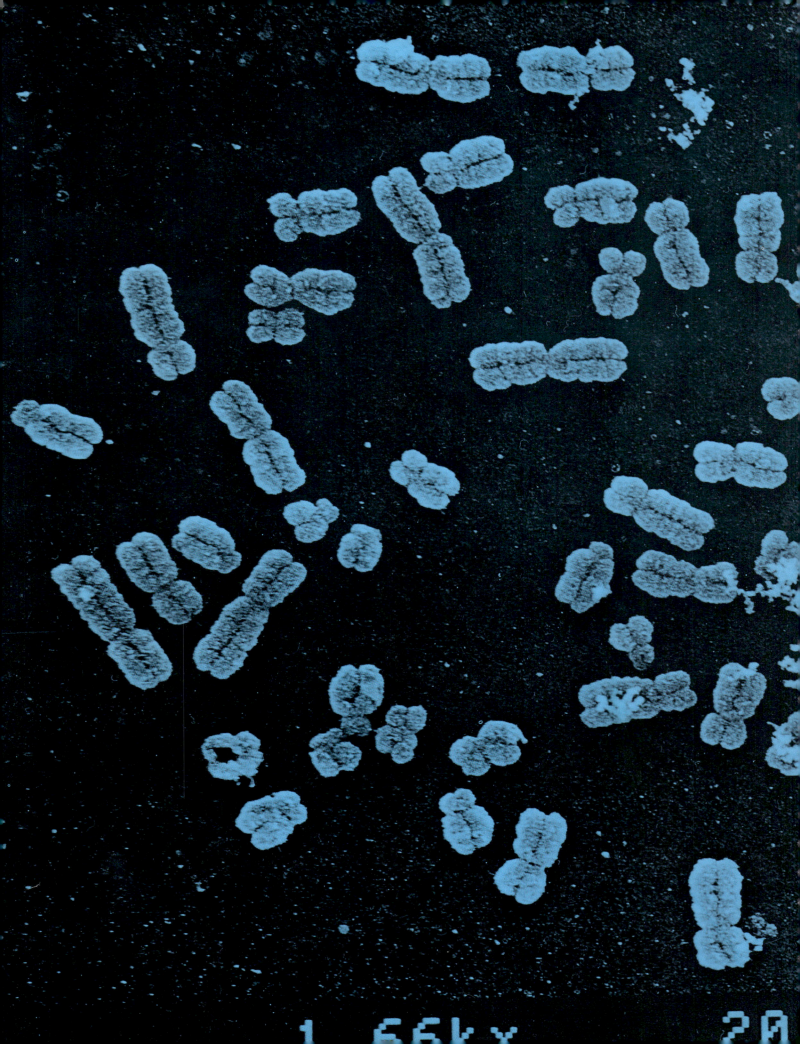

Introduction

For the first time in human history, science has given us the power to alter our own natures. We can do so by genetic engineering: the process by which scientists can change the blueprints that determine the form and function of every living thing. With it we can create new flowers, plants and animals, even new men and women. Genetic engineering could provide the means to eliminate diseases, increase food production, and revolutionise the chemical industry. Many see it as the most important scientific development since the splitting of the atom.

But the new powers bring new questions. Is it right, or sensible, to change life forms that have evolved over millions of years? Might newly engineered organisms escape, harming other forms of life that have no protection against them? And as we learn the genetic causes of many diseases, how do we use the information? To tell someone that he or she may die young because of inherited genes is an appalling responsibility – but have we the right to conceal that information from him or her? The under-standing and control of genetic information raises issues which we have never had to tackle before. This book explains the nature of the genetic revolution, it explores what it means for industry, health and farming, and looks at the dilemmas that have been created.

◁ Human chromosomes are tiny chains that carry packets of information in the nucleus of almost every cell. Visible only through a microscope, they carry all the information needed to make us both human and unique.

What is genetic engineering?

▽ The human body is made up of about ten trillion cells. Inside each cell (1) is a set of 46 chromosomes (2) which consist of coiled fibres (3) made up of spirals of DNA (4) wrapped around proteins. A gene (5) is a portion of this spiral.

All living things are made of cells, tiny compartments a fraction of a millimetre across that can only be seen through a microscope. Cells are the factories of life. They can turn simple chemicals into the proteins that make up our bodies, and they multiply by producing identical copies of themselves. Cells come in millions of different varieties, each with a specific function.

How do cells know what to do? Near the centre of each cell, in the region called the nucleus, are thread-like structures that carry the instructions which the cell follows. These are the chromosomes. All living things have them, though not all have the same number: human beings have 46, mice have 40, tomatoes 24, and the fruit fly only four.

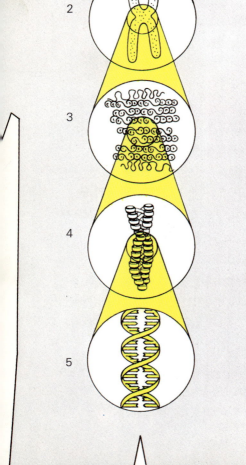

▽ Genetic engineers at work: the practice of genetic engineering involves the insertion of foreign genes from other species into cells. A number of methods can be used. Here an animal cell is being micro-injected with DNA through a very fine syringe, while the cell is held still by the suction tube on the left.

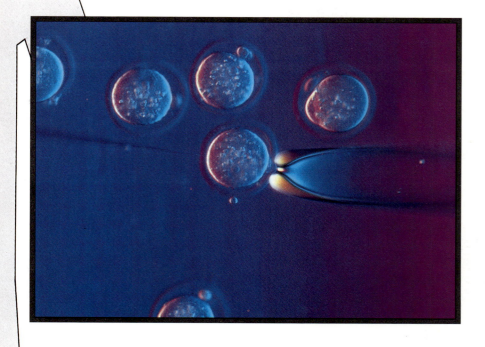

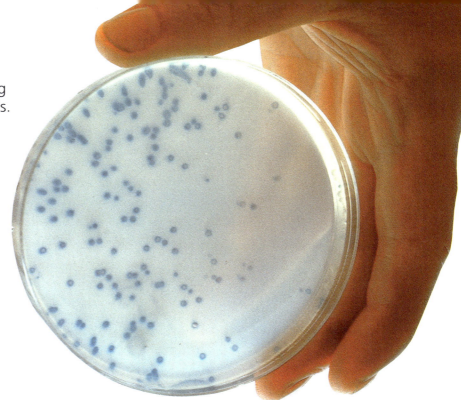

▷ After being genetically altered, dyed virus colonies now containing foreign DNA show up as blue spots.

The mechanisms of inheritance were discovered by a monk, Gregor Mendel, who experimented with garden peas at his monastery in Brno, Czechoslovakia, in 1856. Concentrating on the inheritance of easily identifiable traits like the colour of pea flowers or plant height, Mendel showed that character-istics are inherited from both parent plants . He also showed how some genes responsible for passing on these traits are dominant over others, determining the outcome of any cross. His experiments explained many mysteries of inheritance, but went unnoticed for years.

Inside the chromosomes, the actual information is written in the form of a long corkscrew-shaped molecule called DNA— deoxyribonucleic acid. DNA contains four chemicals called bases — adenine, thymine, cytosine and guanine — which form pairs that are arranged in different orders. It is the ordering of these base pairs that determines the behaviour of the cell. Just as a signal can be sent in Morse code as a series of dots and dashes, so the instructions for the cell are spelled out by the order of the bases along the DNA molecules.

Each human cell contains about three billion pairs of bases. Along the DNA molecule there are sections, ranging from a few bases long to a million or more, that have specific functions. These are genes, whose job it is to provide the blueprints for the thousands of chemicals that the body needs. In genetic engineering, the DNA of a species can be isolated, a short section snipped out and a new section, from a totally different kind of cell, inserted or spliced in. The cell will then be programmed to function differently.

Engineering beginnings

The genes in living things are not fixed for ever. They can change spontaneously, producing strange and sometimes extraordinary mutations. Sometimes these mutations lead to disease and early death; sometimes they are beneficial, helping a species to evolve and survive. Taking advantage of such changes, and using selective breeding to perpetuate them, people have developed the many species of cultivated plants, domestic animals and pets familiar to us all. But it has taken thousands of years for traditional methods to reach this point.

Genetic engineering offers a shortcut. Instead of waiting for natural mutations to alter genes, scientists can now change them for us. The genes responsible for a particular function in one species — disease resistance, say — can be removed and placed in a different species, giving it the same resistance. The implications of these methods are nothing short of revolutionary.

▽ Generations of selective breeding can produce many changes in a species. Every breed of dog, from the sturdy boxer to the dachshund, originated in the wolf. The occurrence of random genetic changes, preserved by cross-breeding, has produced today's range of dog breeds. Rabbits show similar though less dramatic variations. Floppy ears offer no advantage in the wild, so the trait has not thrived in wild rabbits. But this chance variation has been preserved and developed by breeders to create an attractive pet.

In one of the first uses of this technique, cells of the common bacterium *Escherichia coli* (known as *E coli*) were modified by adding the human gene which codes for the protein insulin. Other important proteins, like human growth hormone, can be produced in the same way.

This method is known as recombinant DNA, and was first carried out in 1973. To achieve it, many other discoveries were also necessary. Ways had to be found of cutting DNA at just the right point, of splicing the extra piece into the gene (re-combining DNA, hence the name) and then of reinserting the engineered gene into the cells. Many scientists in laboratories all over the world contributed to the process. Success meant that for the first time it was possible to create in the laboratory new varieties of bacteria, plants and animals unknown in nature, programmed to serve human purposes. There were many benefits and a few risks.

The first triumph of genetic engineering was the production of a hormone called somato-statin, in 1977. It is a small molecule, normally made in the pancreas, and its gene is only 42 bases long, which meant that it was possible to synthesise it chemically, base by base. The synthetic gene was then put into *E coli* bacteria, which produced the hormone.

The story of insulin
One of the most common inherited diseases is diabetes, caused by a failure to control sugar levels in the body. In the 1920s it was found that sufferers lacked the ability to make insulin, normally created in the pancreas and used to reduce sugar levels in the blood. Insulin from animals can be used as a substitute, but diabetics must inject it directly into the bloodstream. Today human insulin can be produced in large quantities by genetically engineered *E coli* bacteria.

Alarm bells

The discovery of the structure of DNA in 1953 and the unravelling of the genetic code in the 1960s were triumphs of scientific understanding. But when in the 1970s the methods for altering DNA were discovered, concern was immediately expressed about the implications. Some people began to question the entire moral basis of the new science.

By changing the genes of plants, animals and human beings, were scientists acquiring godlike powers to determine the future of life on Earth? This could be potentially dangerous, for how could any one individual be wise enough to determine the ultimate effect of a genetic change that might be made? In the wrong hands, genetic engineering might be used to try to produce a super-race, or to generate even more horrible biological weapons. To control it, new organisations would need to be created.

△ During the Second World War, prisoners of the Nazis in Germany were used as guinea-pigs in a series of genetic experiments. One of those responsible was Dr Josef Mengele. Cruel, poorly-conducted, and pointless, these experiments overshadow much of today's debate about genetic engineering.

Ethics was not the only issue; safety was also involved. Might this new power lead to the production of a rogue germ that would escape from the laboratory and wipe out life on Earth? In 1975, at a conference at Asilomar in California, the pioneers of the new science got together to establish guidelines. Rather than waiting for the unforeseen consequences that have followed so many scientific discoveries, they tried to anticipate them. The rules laid down then, subsequently relaxed when it appeared fears had been exaggerated, have controlled genetic engineering and kept it safe.

The guidelines which have been laid down for the control of genetic engineering experiments do two things. They try to make sure that potentially dangerous organisms cannot escape, by specifying the degrees of containment that must be used when doing experiments. And they ensure that the bacteria used in the experiments are very feeble ones that need a lot of coddling to survive. If they were to escape, this means that they could not exist for long in the wild and would quickly die out.

◁ Two sisters, Elizabeth Oscowitz and Perla Ositz, testified at the mock-trial of Dr Josef Mengele during a congress on genetic experiments in 1985. They were the sole survivors of the seven sets of dwarf twins Mengele experimented upon at Auschwitz concentration camp in Poland.

Paul Berg of Stanford University in California was the first to construct a recombinant DNA molecule, for which he shared the 1980 Nobel Prize for Chemistry. Aware of the potential dangers of the technique, he warned in 1974 of the need for new regulations and greater self-control by scientists. Guidelines were brought in and the two principles of physical and biological containment have provided effective safeguards so far.

The laboratory of life

Genetic engineering quickly became big business. The princes of the new industry were the scientists who had made the discoveries. With money from private investment, genetic engineering companies began springing up in the mid-1970s. The main centre was in San Francisco, where the new companies Cetus and Genentech based themselves on discoveries made at local universities. By 1980, reflecting excitement in the new science, investors bought eagerly into the industry. In 1977 Genentech had been launched with a capital of $1 million; by 1980, Wall Street valued it at over half a billion dollars. Share values soared and a few scientists became millionaires. But the early financial promise was exaggerated. The companies have been successful, but it has taken them longer than expected to become profitable.

▽ Experiments in genetic engineering must be carried out in conditions of isolation or containment, to prevent the release of potentially dangerous organisms. The degree of containment depends on the type of experiment, with the most care being used when the risks are considered greatest. Some scientists consider that risks have been exaggerated, and that science has been held up by the imposition of controls. Without such guidelines, public opposition to genetic engineering might have been much stronger.

▽ At the Pasteur Institute in Paris, a scientist sets up a powerful light microscope in preparation for the delicate work of micro-injection. Using miniature instruments he will manipulate the cells while observing them through the microscope. Immobilising a single cell with a suction probe, the experimenter will introduce foreign DNA into the nucleus with a second, finer probe. With such techniques scientists at the institute hope to further their research into cancer and the genes which induce some forms of the disease.

Today the older drug companies in Europe and the United States have taken the lead, collaborating with or taking over the genetic engineering companies. The rush to make money from genetic engineering angered some people. Should discoveries part-funded by public money be used to make some scientists rich? Is there a danger that the secrecy which commercial companies demand will stifle the free flow of ideas that made the original discoveries possible? Most scientists believe that commercialisation was inevitable and that the industry will continue to flourish, though more soberly.

▷ ICI is one of the well-established drug companies in Europe now involved in genetic engineering.

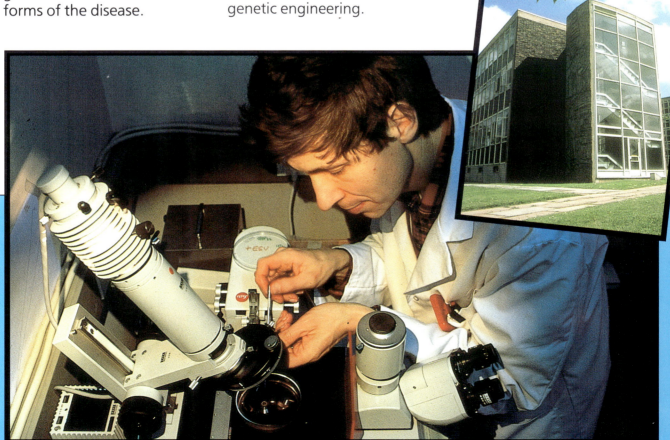

Bring on the clones

One of the favourite nightmares of science fiction writers is the creation of an army of identical men, using the technique of cloning. It is likely to remain no more than a nightmare, but cloning is real enough. It is used to multiply engineered cells a millionfold so that they can produce a far greater output. It is also used in agriculture to produce identical copies of plants or animals.

Cloning in plants is not new. Every time a gardener takes a cutting, he or she is producing a clone: a plant identical in every respect to its single parent. But some plants, palm trees for example, will not regenerate from cuttings. To clone them, cells are grown in a culture of nutrient material, multiplied, and encouraged to grow into thousands of new plants.

△ Seven calves born in January 1988 in Houston, Texas, were among the first animals ever to be cloned. Their father was a prize bull, their mother an equally valuable cow, whose fertilised eggs were split and divided among 16 foster mothers. Only eight resulted in calves, one stillborn. Soon this technique may be used for breeding high-quality herds.

▽ The nightmare of cloned humans — an army of identical super-warriors, for example — seems remote and unlikely. If the technical problems could be solved, it would still require the same number of women willing to act as surrogate mothers. It is also hard to see what would be achieved by cloning men. It takes all sorts to make an army.

The cloning of animals is much less developed. The idea is to produce as many identical copies as possible of a champion animal. To do so, the embryo of, say, a calf produced by breeding two prize animals is removed from its mother a few days after fertilisation. Using miniature surgical tools, the nuclei from this cell cluster are removed and inserted into non-fertilised eggs of ordinary cows. These new embryos are then reimplanted into foster mothers, who give birth to identical calves. The limitations are that foster mothers must be found to bring the embryos to term – one reason why human cloning seems unlikely – and that a limited number, not thousands, can be produced in each generation.

▽ Growing cells in nutrient culture provides a new way of cloning plants. It has been used in Britain and France to clone palm trees, which cannot be reproduced from cuttings. Here Gilles Chastel, a French nurseryman, examines young palms cloned in a test-tube and planted out.

△ Cloning animals involves removing the nuclei from the cells of a fertilised egg when it has reached the 16- or 32-cell stage. The nuclei are then placed in unfertilised eggs from other mothers and implanted in their wombs.

Genetic engineering and bacteria factories

The workhorse of genetic engineering is the common bacterium called *Escherichia coli*, which normally inhabits the human gut, amongst other places. Bacteria are single-celled organisms found in plants, animals and human beings. Some cause disease but the vast majority of them are harmless. They contain one large circular strand of DNA which controls the way they function, together with smaller DNA molecules, also circular, called plasmids, which have the ability to move between cells.

△ To avoid contamination, and to minimise the dangers of escapes and possible contamination, genetic experiments are often done inside glove boxes like the one pictured here. This ensures a sterile, inactive, dry and dust-free atmosphere. To conduct his experiment, the scientist puts his hands into the gloves which are attached to the front of the box.

16

▷ Through an electron microscope the circular DNA plasmids of *E coli* can be seen. Foreign DNA can be spliced into one of these plasmids, then reintroduced into the bacterium, where it produces the substance coded for by the piece of foreign DNA.

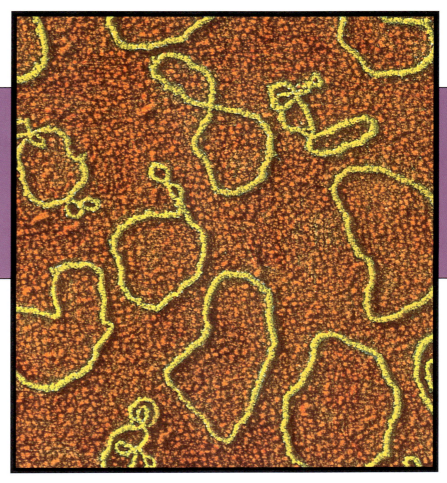

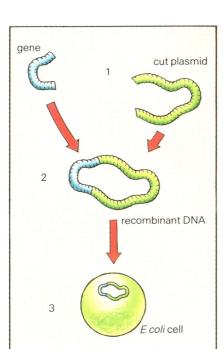

A small section of DNA that codes for the desired protein is isolated. A plasmid of *E coli* is cut, using a special chemical called an enzyme (1). This leaves the plasmid with "sticky ends" which combine with the piece of foreign DNA (2). Then the engineered plasmid is put back into *E coli* cells (3), which are grown in a nutrient material.

Plasmids appear to be nature's way of exchanging genes between bacterial cells, but genetic engineers use them as vehicles for carrying foreign pieces of DNA into *E coli* cells. Receiving their new instructions from the fragments of foreign DNA, the *E coli* cells become miniature factories for producing the proteins coded for by the DNA. Insulin is one protein which is now manufactured through this technique. Once cells with the right genes in them have been made, they are provided with a comfortable home, in the form of a nutrient broth at the right temperature. They can grow very rapidly, dividing into two every 20 minutes or so – which means that in ten hours a single cell has become a billion cells, each producing the useful protein that the foreign genes code for. Finally, the protein is extracted from the broth for use.

Genetic disease

Read any copy of any newspaper carefully enough and you will find spelling mistakes that have slipped through. The same is true of our genes. Among the 100,000 genes that determine the characteristics of every individual are at least six or seven that have gone wrong. Usually such errors do not matter; we carry them through life without even noticing. But for some people, the inheritance of genetic defects from one of their parents means a life foreshortened by disease or affected by mental or physical disability.

Genetic diseases vary enormously in frequency. Some are extremely rare, like Tay-Sachs disease, which affects only one child in 200,000. Others are much more common, like cystic fibrosis (one in 2,000) muscular dystrophy (one in 5,000) or the most common of all, Down's syndrome, which affects one birth in 650. Some diseases are caused by a fault in a single gene, others (like Down's syndrome) by changes in entire chromosomes.

The effects of some diseases are apparent from the moment of birth, while others only appear in childhood or emerge much later in life. For some there are treatments, for others nothing at all can be done at the present time.

Queen Victoria was a carrier of haemophilia, passing the condition on to her children, who took it into the royal houses of Europe through marriage. "Our poor family seems persecuted by this awful disease," she wrote.

Thalassaemia A disease common among peoples of Mediterranean origin, in which the red blood cells break up. It is passed on when two carriers of the recessive gene that causes the disease have children. Carriers of the gene have an immunity to malaria.

Duchenne muscular dystrophy Caused by a fault in the X chromosome, the gene responsible has been identified. It affects boys, causing wasting of the muscles and death by the age of about 20. Prenatal diagnosis can now identify the faulty gene.

Haemophilia Another disease caused by the X chromosome, of which girls have two, boys only one. In girls with one faulty chromosome, the other makes up for it; boys suffer from blood that will not clot. They can survive with blood infusions.

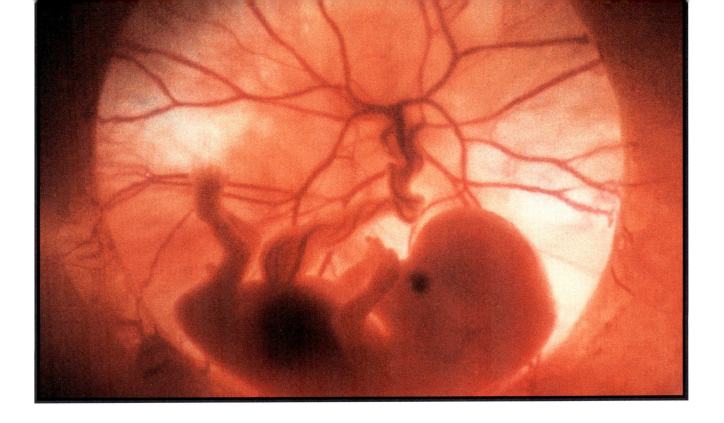

Today at least the actual defects that cause many diseases have been identified. Mothers known to be at risk of having babies with genetic disease can have tests early in pregnancy, and may be offered abortion if the results are positive. Testing for thalassaemia, a blood disease which kills children in infancy or early adulthood, has reduced the number of such children born on the island of Sardinia by 70 per cent in under ten years. In the future better treatments, or even the repair of defective genes, may be possible through genetic engineering.

△ A human embryo at 11 weeks. Prenatal screening of embryos can spare enormous unhappiness. If women know they are at risk of having a baby with a genetic disease, a small sample of tissue can be removed from the embryo early in pregnancy and analysed for genetic faults. This can pick up some diseases and give the women a choice of having an abortion.

Cystic fibrosis A disease caused by a recessive gene which was identified in 1989. One in four children of carriers suffers from the disease, in which thick mucus accumulates in air passages in the lungs, causing breathing difficulties and infections.

Sickle cell anaemia One in ten black people in the United States is a carrier of this disease, in which red blood cells take on a sickle shape. Damaged cells are removed from the blood-stream by the spleen, causing anaemia. Most victims die by the age of 20.

Huntington's chorea A disease for years unrecognised, because it emerges only in middle age. Victims suffer jerky movements and dementia, and ultimately die. In the past sufferers were suspected of being possessed by witches, or of being alcoholics.

Medical applications

By the time this baby has grown up, many of the diseases that threaten it through life may have been conquered through the use of genetic engineering techniques. New medicines and vaccines will be developed against illnesses, while inherited disease may be treated by gene therapy – replacing faulty genes with sound ones. Cancer and heart disease, the greatest killers in the West, may be conquered.

The practice of medicine is likely to be transformed in the next generation by the use of genetic engineering to create new drugs and vaccines. When a body is attacked by an infectious organism, it produces antibodies to kill it. These antibodies are produced as a reaction to molecules called antigens from the invader. Vaccines work by "teaching" the body to produce the right antibodies to fight a disease without actually having the ailment.

Typhoid, dysentery and cholera – Major killers in the Third World, more controllable now, but better vaccines could save millions of lives.

Heart attacks – Genetic studies may determine how likely attacks are; genetically engineered drugs already available as treatment.

Hepatitis – Vaccine available now, produced by genetically engineered yeasts. Within five years all forms of the disease could be prevented.

Injuries – Sticking plasters may be made with a special material on them to hasten the regrowth of skin. This material occurs naturally but can be made in large amounts by genetic engineering.

Cancer – Antibodies could be used to carry killer drugs or radioisotopes direct to the tumour as "magic bullets"

Genetically engineered yeasts can now be used to produce antigens to use as vaccines. Another approach is to take the organism that causes a disease and identify which part of its gene is lethal. A vaccine against cholera has been developed by producing a strain of the cholera organism that lacks the gene that produces the poison. A similar method may also work for typhoid. Viral diseases like the common cold may be treated by interferon, the body's own defence, produced in large amounts by genetic engineering. It ought soon to be possible for scientists to manufacture materials like epidermal growth factor, which helps wounds heal more quickly, or insulin-like growth factor which might be used to treat arthritis.

Diabetes – More controllable now, using pig insulin and genetically engineered human insulin. In future, transplants of the organs that produce insulin should be possible.

Bones – Material called "insulin-like growth factor" could help bones mend, or treat bone disease.

AIDS – Vaccines to protect against the spread of the AIDS virus are being developed, using genetic engineering techniques. Better drugs to treat victims of the virus are also being tested now.

On the farm

Farmers want better crops, bigger harvests, and animals that grow more quickly to marketable size. Genetic engineering can provide them. But it can also do things farmers have never imagined. On a farm near Edinburgh there is a flock of apparently normal sheep. These sheep, however, have had their genes altered so that their milk contains a clotting agent normally found only in human blood. The gene that codes for this protein has been inserted into the sheep's gene, so that the sheep produces the clotting agent in its milk. The agent can be extracted from the milk and used by medical science.

▽ A genetically altered super-mouse runs beside a mouse of normal size. Supermice were produced by taking the growth hormone gene from rats and introducing it into mice. The mice grew more quickly and analyses showed that their bodies contained 100 to 800 times as much growth hormone as ordinary mice. The experiment has implications for farm animals, though there is still a lot which has to be learned.

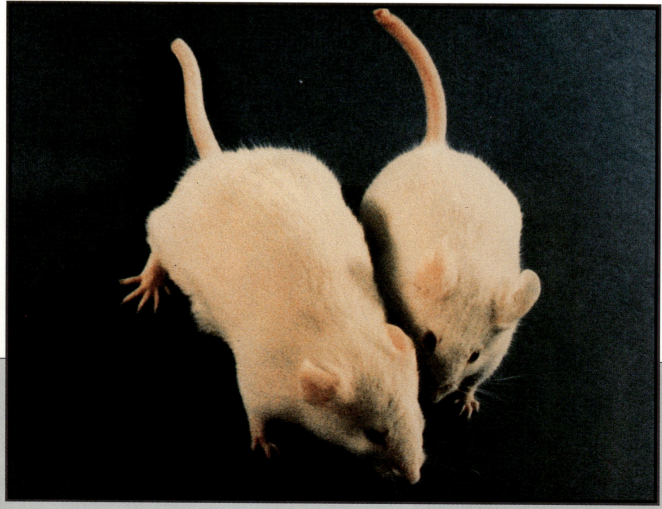

Plants have been improved by adding genes from unrelated plants that confer resistance to disease. In 1990 the gene from a pea that confers resistance to Colorado beetle and tuber root moth was isolated and added to potatoes. A great prize would be a strain of wheat that could take up nitrogen from the air, as legume crops like peas already can, thereby reducing the need for nitrogen fertilisers.

Animals reared for their meat might be improved by giving them extra growth hormone, to create a breed of fast-growing pigs or beef cattle. It worked in mice, but much less well in pigs, which suffered crippling arthritis. Critics argue that such experiments are wrong, exploiting animals and perhaps condemning them to a short and unpleasant life.

▽ Self-lighting tobacco: the gene that makes fireflies glow in the dark has been introduced into tobacco plants, producing plants that glow. The object was to provide a tool for studying the expression of genes in plants, rather than improving the tobacco plant. The gene that produces the protein luciferase in fireflies was isolated, transferred to a bacterium, and then injected into plant tissues. The same technique can be used for transferring other genes, those that provide resistance to disease, for example.

▽ Sheep at the Institute for Animal Physiology and Genetics Research, near Edinburgh, carry the human gene for producing a blood clotting agent. The agent appears in the sheep's milk, being collected below.

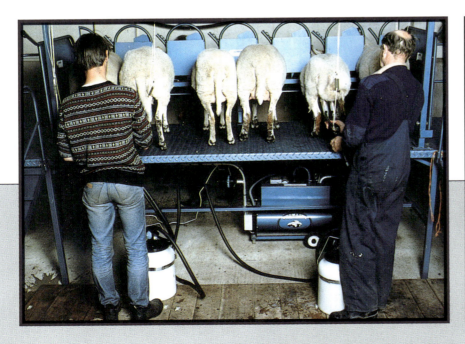

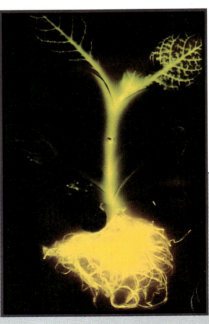

Mapping men . . .

In 1986, at a cost of several billion dollars, a group of scientists world-wide launched a project aimed at working out the order of all three billion base pairs that make up the human genetic blueprint, or genome. This controversial scheme is headed in America by Dr James Watson, co-discoverer of the structure of DNA.

Its defenders claim that it will give us the key to understanding humankind within 15 years. It will unlock the working of the brain, the mysteries of inherited disease, and explain why some people are predisposed to conditions like cancer or heart disease. Its critics say it is a waste of money.

▷ The screen displays a small fraction of one human gene among the 100,000 that will have to be sequenced in the human genome project. Located on chromosome six, it is a gene which determines the behaviour of the immune system, and it was originally sequenced because of its importance in transplant surgery. The sequence consists of a series of letters, T, G, C and A, representing thymine, guanine, cytosine and adenine, the four bases whose ordering is the language of the genetic code.

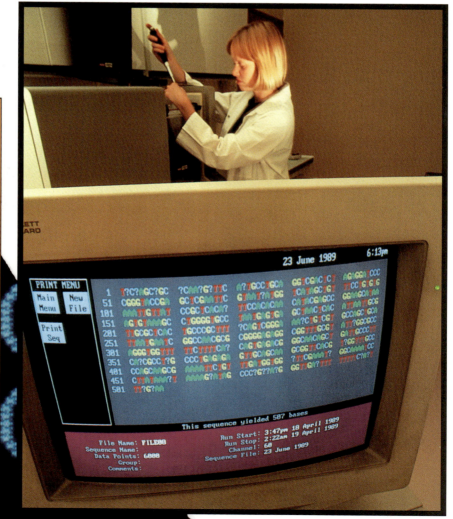

and women

So far, scientists attempting to read the human genome have concentrated on small sections important in genetic disease or in coding for certain key proteins. They have so far sequenced only one thousandth of the entire genome, and have found that most of the three billion base pairs appear to have no useful function at all; only five per cent of the genome seems to be actual genes, the function of the rest being at present unclear. That, and the cost of the project, have caused it to be scaled down. The latest idea is to develop a "map" of the whole genome, locating sections of interest and sequencing them, but postponing the sequencing of all three billion base pairs.

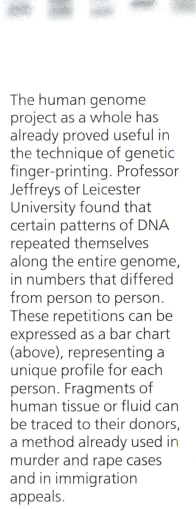

▽ The magnitude of the task of mapping the human genome can be imagined from the length of this computer printout analysis of part of the sequencing of base pairs along a molecule of plant DNA. The human genome contains three billion of such base pairs, many of whose role is obscure.

The human genome project as a whole has already proved useful in the technique of genetic finger-printing. Professor Jeffreys of Leicester University found that certain patterns of DNA repeated themselves along the entire genome, in numbers that differed from person to person. These repetitions can be expressed as a bar chart (above), representing a unique profile for each person. Fragments of human tissue or fluid can be traced to their donors, a method already used in murder and rape cases and in immigration appeals.

Fears and dangers

▽ Jeremy Rifkin, the American author and campaigner, has become the leading critic of genetic engineering. He believes that humans will pay a heavy price for genetic experimentation, reducing ourselves to the status of a technologically designed species. Through a series of court actions, Rifkin and his Foundation on Economic Trends delayed the introduction of genetically engineered organisms into the wild. In the long run, he warns, genetics will turn into eugenics, with people deciding which genes are undesirable. No-one, he says, has the right to tamper with human genes, for they are what makes us human.

The first fears provoked by genetic engineering turned out to be exaggerated. The strain of *E coli* used by the scientists cannot survive long outside the laboratory, so concern about a "super-bug" being released has faded.

But what about organisms that are designed to be used outside laboratories, like the new plants produced by genetic engineering? The risk here is that the plants will not behave as their designers intended, and may damage other species in unpredictable ways, as the introduction of foreign plants and animals has done in some countries in the past. All nations engaged in this kind of research have set up regulatory authorities or committees whose job it is to assess the risks. So far the system has worked, but the numbers of organisms released is still quite small (16 in Britain by the end of 1989). Continued vigilance will be needed.

Genetic engineering also raises moral and ethical issues. It may be uncontroversial to modify the "bad" gene that causes diabetes, but it is usually difficult to judge whether a particular gene is bad. For example, some children become short-sighted before the age of ten, almost certainly as a result of a particular gene. But such children are also more intelligent than average. Some critics fear that the new powers will be used to "correct" short-sight, left-handedness, or even skin colour. What if we can identify the genes that contribute to a high IQ? Genetic engineering could become a form of eugenics, a programme aimed at improving the species, such as the Nazis had. There are no easy answers to these dilemmas. Scientific discoveries often have the power to do harm as well as good. Only by understanding and controlling them can we be sure that the worst nightmares will be prevented.

▽ When the first experiments in genetic engineering took place, anxieties about them in the United States were widespread. In Cambridge, Massachusetts, public pressure delayed the opening of a new laboratory, while a meeting of the US Academy of Sciences was picketed (below) by a group called the People's Business Commission. They protested that private companies were behind the experiments and were trying to get patents on living things and profit from them. Today the protests have largely died down as a result of restraint by scientists, effective controls by governments and lack of evidence that the worst fears of critics were justified.

The future

The industry of genetic engineering is still in its infancy. In the next 20 years it is likely to prove as influential as nuclear energy or the computer revolution. From the womb to the grave, we will understand more about what makes us tick than we ever have before. The random nature of inheritance – the lottery of life in which we all have to take our chances – may for the first time come within human control.

Thousands of new drugs, plants, animals and chemical products will be made by genetically engineered cells, and will become available for a price. Diseases that have dogged humans for thousands of years may be controlled or even eliminated. These new powers are awe-inspiring, even a little frightening.

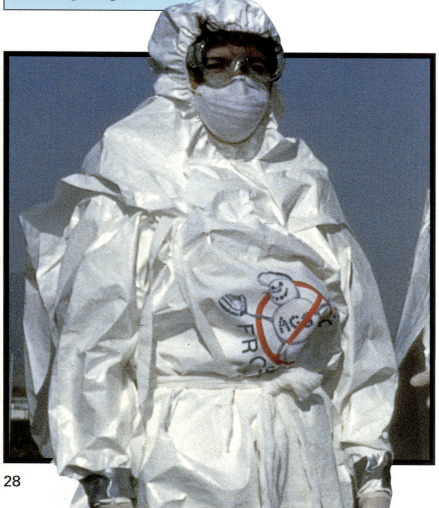

◁ In 1984 two American groups proposed an experiment designed to protect crops from frost. Ice forms on leaves in cold weather around a protein produced by a bacterium. If the bacterium were replaced by one which could not make this protein, ice might not form and the plants would survive. Protestors argued that it was dangerous to release genetically engineered organisms into the environment. The experiments were stopped, and only finally went ahead in 1987 when crops were sprayed by men clad in protective clothing (left). In the end, after all the controversy the results were unimpressive.

New laws will be needed to make sure these powers are not abused. Legislation covering the use of embryos in research has shown the way, but laws will also be needed to protect the individual from the consequences of the human genome project. If everybody's genes can be read, how will those with "faulty" genes find jobs, marry, or buy life insurance? These issues have hardly been discussed, much less solved.

The potential benefits of genetic engineering, like those of other scientific advances, seem greatly to exceed the threats posed. So far, the work has been handled well by the scientists involved, who are aware of the ethical implications of their work. Given care, there is no reason why this should not continue.

Dame Mary Warnock, Mistress of Girton College, Cambridge, gave her name in 1984 to an influential British report into *in vitro* (test-tube) fertilisation. The report recommended that growing embryos in test-tubes for more than 14 days should be a criminal offence, and this is now the law in Britain. In Germany an even stricter law, banning genetic engineering of human embryos, was enacted in October 1990.

▽ After *in vitro* fertilisation a fertilised egg is reimplanted in the mother's womb. Research on fertilised eggs which are not reimplanted is now illegal in Britain after 14 days. Similar ethical debates surround genetic engineering.

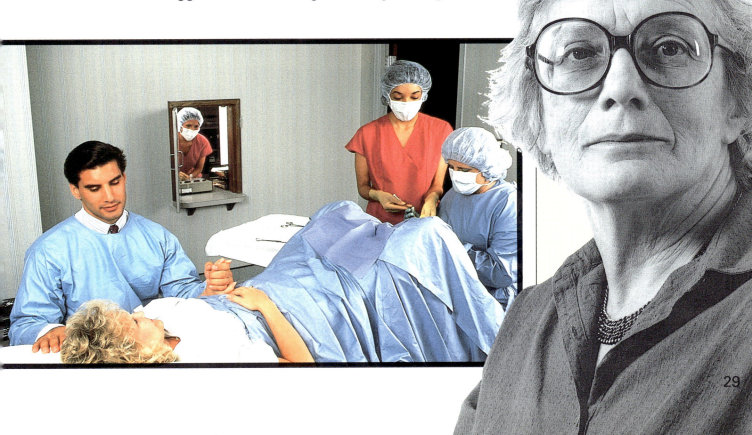

Chronology

1871 Discovery of DNA by the Swiss biochemist Friedrich Mieschler, in the sperm of trout from the river Rhine. He calls the material "nuclein".

1879 The German biochemist Albrecht Kossel isolates from DNA four nitrogen-containing compounds, which he names adenine, guanine, cytosine and thymine.

1938 Alexander Todd (later Lord Todd) begins work at Manchester on the chemistry of the nucleic acids, showing how they are bound together.

1953 Francis Crick and James Watson, working at Cambridge, propose a double helix structure for DNA, based on X-ray crystallography.

1966 The complete genetic code, by which the four bases code for proteins, is established for the first time.

1973 Fragments of foreign DNA are inserted into plasmid DNA by Paul Berg at Stanford.

1974 Berg and others, in a letter to *Science*, call for a worldwide moratorium or ban on recombinant DNA experiments until their safety can be ensured.

1975 The moratorium ends.

The conference at Asilomar establishes safety guidelines.

1977 Genentech, the first company to make use of recombinant DNA technology, sets up in business in San Francisco.

1978 Genentech produces somatostatin, a hormone, the first human protein to be manufactured by DNA technology.

1981 Sickle cell anaemia is diagnosed prenatally, by the analysis of the DNA taken from an embryo.

1982 Supermice are produced by inserting the gene for rat growth hormone into fertilised mouse eggs.

1985 Cetus, in California, develop a method for identifying and amplifying sequences of DNA very quickly. It revolutionises the process of sequencing DNA.

1986 Human genome project launched by James Watson.

1989 The gene that causes cystic fibrosis is discovered by Lap-Chee Tsui of the Toronto Hospital for Sick Children and Francis Collins of the University of Michigan.

1990 Plans are made for the first human gene therapy, on children with weak immune systems.

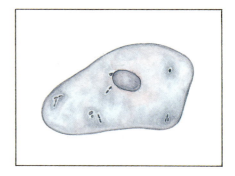

Microbes have been engineered to create pest-fighting viruses, and bacteria to speed animal digestion.

The colour of petunias has been changed from pink to brick red by genetic engineers in German universities.

Softening in tomatoes is caused by an enzyme which has been "switched off" by scientists in Britain.

Pest-resistant potatoes have been developed by incorporating the gene in peas that resists certain diseases.

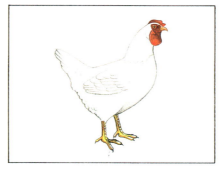

Chickens may be engineered to become resistant to salmonella infection and to lay more eggs.

Mice with human cancer have been engineered in America to aid research into the cancer-causing genes.

Sheep whose milk contains the human blood-clotting Factor IX have now been developed in Britain.

Carp eggs were microinjected with growth hormones from fast-growing rainbow trout to make fast-growing carp.

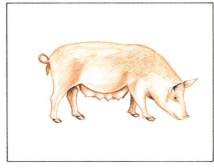

Pigs were given growth hormone to make them extra-meaty, though tests so far have not been a success.

Antibodies Proteins made by the body to fight off germs

Antigens Foreign molecules against which antibodies mobilise

Bacteria Single-celled organisms which are found in living things and in the air, water and soil

Bases The four chemicals that make up the rungs of the double helix ladder of DNA

Chromosomes Thread-like structures in the nucleus of the cell that carry genetic information

DNA Deoxyribonucleic acid, the double helix molecule that is the basis of all life on Earth

Enzyme A protein capable of speeding up or slowing down chemical reactions

Gene Section of DNA, responsible for providing the information for making one protein

Genome The total complement of genes in a cell or an individual

Plasmids Small rings of DNA in bacteria

Proteins The structural molecules of life

Vaccines Drugs that confer resistance to disease

Index

Photographic Credits
Front and back cover and pages 6, 7 top, 9, 12, 13, 16, 17, 19 top, 24 left and right, 25 left and 29: Science Photo Library; pages 4-5 and 19 bottom: Biophoto Associates; pages 7 bottom, 10 bottom, 11 and 18: Popperfoto; page 8 left: Hutchison Library; page 8 right: F. Killerby; pages 10 top, 14-15, 15 middle and bottom, 22, 23 right, 25 right and 28: Frank Spooner Pictures; page 13 inset: ICI Corporate Slide Bank; page 14-15: Roger Vlitos; pages 20-21: Catherine Bradley; page 23 left: Agricultural and Food Research Council; pages 26, 26-27 and 29 right: Camera Press.

PRINTED IN BELGIUM BY
proost
INTERNATIONAL BOOK PRODUCTION